AF228060

Driving at Night in October

"Driving at Night in October" © 2018 J.L. Cooper

Cover illustration © 2018 Cameron J. Cooper
Author photo by Betty Cooper
Layout by Sam Cowan

Published by Five Warblers Press
PO Box #3092, Citrus Heights, CA 95611-3092
fivewarblers.wordpress.com

First Edition
ISBN 978-1-7326631-3-8

All rights reserved. No part of this book may be reproduced or transmitted in any form or by any means, electronic or mechanical, including photocopying, recording, or by any information storage and retrieval system without the written permission of the publisher, except where permitted by law.

Driving at Night in October

Poetry by
J.L. Cooper

Carmichael, CA / 2018

Acknowledgments

I'm grateful to the editors of the following journals where these poems have been accepted for publication.

"Driving at Night in October"
Grand Prize in Poetry: *Crosswinds Poetry Journal Contest,* 2018
Judge: Lloyd Schwartz, Pulitzer winner in criticism

"Eulogy With Paper Lamps"
Finalist: 2017, Joy Harjo Poetry Contest
Cutthroat, Issue 23, 2018

"Clinical Note Template for Men in Therapy"
Finalist: New Millennium 45th Poetry Prize
To be published in *New Millennium Writings Anthology,* 2019

"The Ropes on Scalloway Pier"
The Comstock Review (to be published in 2018)

Recognition

A version of this collection, under a different title, was a finalist in the 2017 Jessie Bryce Niles Chapbook Contest at *The Comstock Review.*

Table of Contents

Note on the Kitchen Counter

I hope you dreamed in color.
Join me out back for tea.
Earl Grey is stately waiting,
Black Peach, the name beguiles.

It's Irish Breakfast for me,
there's more in the cabinet drawer.
Take the path between the privet
and my favorite red hibiscus.

Go past the broken tree house
the children loved so much.
If you spot a pear in the orchard,
bring it for us to share. Amazing –

the same arbor, same climbing rose.
You'll find me in the morning light.
There's something I need to tell you.
Mostly, we'll laugh, I promise.

Supergirl

Here you come; you and your
sundrenched ways, wondering
what your superpower will be.

Maybe cavorting, or the way
a runner always looks up
when the race is finished,

pouring in sweat and relief,
heaving like a bear. You can't
easily name it; it doesn't work

that way. Your power is known
to hide, you see it looking back,
exchanging curiosity and facts,

daring imagination. You
and your deep-seeking ways
come around in little circles.

You've turned a fallen tree
into a palace full of mirrors.
Whatever is at your feet

can speak: mustard fields,
ferns aglow, moss still damp
from the remnant night.

The Unexpected Closeness of Wind

Silent across the plains
a prescient Midwest wind

strolls in – long legs, lifting
your eyes to the seduction

you've needed. This is when
you dream of being a leaf

relinquishing your moisture,
cracking apart in her wind arms,

tumbling in an autumn field
past dormant vines, past roses

once crimson, now rust,
chasing a lowering sun.

It makes you remember
the closeness of absence,

the alertness of presence;
all your dreams and burdens

crumbling and rolling
silent across the plains.

A Little Observation

On a hot afternoon
getting out of the pool
my wife said to me

you're the only one
I've ever met
who lets water

dry on your face
not using a towel.
You just sit in the sun

offering yourself
to the heat of day,
the warm wind,

until the water's gone.
I said *it feels natural,*
a reverent rising,

a kind of elevation,
and I don't want
to interfere.

But her comment
gave me pause
because normally

I'm quite impatient
when it comes
to life on land.

Before She Had Words

My granddaughter found water.
Her tiny hands made porous cups
in a feast of readiness, studying
its feel and texture. Next she made
a waterfall, astonished when it
danced down her sleeve, lush
in liquid gravity, fresh as hay.

This is how she bends the world:
riddled by dragonfly wings, catching
the scent of gardenias, filling a yellow
bucket by the smallest portions.

Wisdom rose in her hungry eyes.
She held a cup of water high
to see it from below; an offering
I thought, this one not for pouring.

A camellia captured her mind,
a tree and next a shovel. The quails
saw the miracle too, from the top
of the old brown fence. A portrait

made haste in the heart. A girl
on a bench with her cup; a gift
of water, a quiet grandfather,
everything full and glistening.

The Ropes on Scalloway Pier

I met a Scottish woman who lived
along the cliffs. She wouldn't let me
take her photo, and lived in otherness.

She thought of complications, saying
various things in various ways; like
you can't photograph wind or worries,

and these are my provinces, you see.
She wouldn't be framed in my aspirations.
No, she said, *I don't like my likeness.*

She wasn't one for this or that, not
one I'd find in a box of photos, thirty
years hence. She had an odd solution:

that I venture alone some amber
evening, out to Scalloway Pier,
with gulls that call to a fishing boat

coming in with a brimming haul.
Then forget the gulls, the boat,
the shouts of men and the salted air,

that I'd find her in the coiled ropes,
in their turns and braids and soft
persuasions, waiting to be called.

The Brahms Conundrum

What you may not learn in college
is how Forrest Gander reads poetry,
asking the air for words, exquisitely
pausing, looking at the back wall
as if an answer might cast itself
in bold block letters that only he
can read; the forgotten sentence
that changes the river's course.

I turned, searching for the source,
but the back row was scattered
with indifferent students, playing
their numb video games, thumbs
and fingers flying, with earphones
drowning possibilities. A woman
slept in the corner, perhaps
in grief, like she'd broken up
with a first love, and didn't know
the poems he read were also
meant for her. Beside her was a
pensive man, serious and jittery,
scribbling with fearsome fury;
a story of rage, a pressured hope,
an angry prayer he dared to know.

We're animals at a watering hole
in Rwanda, with night sounds
clutching the air. I'm thinking
of my father trying to share
with me his love of Brahms.

What a tearful thing for a father
to see that his son couldn't mend
himself in the same long tones
where he found his reverie.

It's the oldest trouble of all;
the Brahms Conundrum
I suppose; the delayed gift,
the bridge across generations.
Oh, how I love him now.

A Season Worth of Green

How easily we planted
a season worth of green,
standing near our roses
in a dream where one
can speak. Unwashed
memories earn this from
new crimson lips;

*find what I am to you
or pass. I won't come
in another form, I'm merely
a crimson rose. Three days
and I am gone.*

Days have turned to decades
but were we ever wise?
In bed when sleep is near,
I reach and bring her closer,
back to our turning ways.

Her tone alone casts me
on her shore, unguarded
by sleepy eyes. We're bare
against the curtains, aware
of the drift of time.

Salt was all I tasted, but wind
was what I feared. Tenacious,
our defiance, written in lines
of prose, in corners of our eyes.

Hands Across a Hickory Table

I'm right across from you,
    realizing
you might put it differently,
saying closeness is side-by-side
like the grain in our hickory table.

I've been thinking too much
    of opposites,
of bridges and ways across.
You might put it differently, saying
our hands must find the wood.

Of course the eyes will know.
    Speak again
of grain, how it once was hidden
inside a tree, how water flowed
vertically in xylem. We didn't see

the cut, the truck that carried it
    from the forest. Now, before us,
this beautiful grain exposed.
You're the one bringing water
and I'm but a hickory sapling.

Bend

sunflowers bend
heavy with their lives
rain is coming

Zinnias

zinnias, seeking sun,
shade the stepping-stones
I surrender

Path

azaleas watch over
the garden path
relentless white

A Gathering of Sighs

I see your sighs were sacrificed,
never rising to a voice. You fought
for every inward breath while all
your sighs drifted, exhausted,
in a fog that wouldn't clear.

You didn't know of summer winds
that found your trace and carried
it north to a cleansing redwood
forest that sweetens every breath
with a touch of innocent longing.

This should be simple, like taking
morning air, but there were rules,
or so you were told, and places
you weren't allowed to visit.

The sighs are restless tonight,
rustling the leaves in a breeze.
They'll come in sleep or when
you gaze in a mirror, gathering
in formless wonder. Each has
a name, a song, a tremulous
piercing truth. They're back, as if
from war, waiting to come home
if only you will have them.

The Curious Joys of Nanny

Inspired by a photograph, 1904, by Jacques Lartigue, at age 8:
Nanny Dudu and Balloon.

A balloon is suspended in air –
a nanny threw it there.
A boy with camera begs –
throw it again, but higher.

A conspiracy of light, I say,
as the boy caught the scene
on camera, when motion
was hard to stop.

Nestled by a hedge, nanny
wears her soiled apron;
her face so round and lit,
hands ascending, as if
she's just released a boy
to the world while she
remains behind; keeper
of gravity, wise in a child's
way, like the child was her own.

Relief is on her face, something
relinquished there. One day
the boy will lose his favorite ball,
over the hedge, down the road,
and he won't think of nanny at all –
until a wheel falls off his car,
or the sphere of moon rises full
in a troubled autumn sky. He sees
that he is lost, and needs to come
back down. Then he remembers
youth – so like a balloon to drift;
wondering where she is now?

How many times did she play
the pirate, hiding in curtains
and shrubs? What potion
of lavender and salts helped her
suffer his irritations?

If you find the old picture,
cover the balloon with your
hand. You'll see her clearly
that way - her willing play,
her eagerness - to chase
the moons of Jupiter.

It's a conspiracy of light I say.
So like a garden to provide
a hedge; juniper, I think.

It was such a brilliant garden,
destined for black-and-white.

(Photo: *The Art of Photography*, Time Life Books, NY,
1971, p.187)

Driving at Night in October

We know this familiar road at night,
leaning into curves, headlights scowling.
It's treacherous to leave our lane.

We know of ditches, boulders, a gravel pit,
it's a wonder how calm we are. Like we've
got an agreement to keep the story going.

It's not the story of the shadow of the tree
falling across our moods, not the seasonal
variations of light. And it can't be the burst

of wind that makes the dandelions unravel.
Certainly not the man/woman conundrum.
If I were Houdini, and you, just now,

Mrs. Dalloway, we'd have a riveting talk
about the curious company we keep,
driving at night in October. Bright fresh

thoughts circle us in the dark. Ironic,
their source so puzzling. We wonder
why the sun won't have them.

*Clinical Note Template for Men in Therapy (Expand
as Necessary)*

Now in our ______ year, we sail in (circle one) turbulent/
calm/turquoise seas. We used to talk of labor and construction,
but we've left the sandstone gorges and ruined cities. We've
left the palaces, overgrown by vines. We're aware of childhood
treasures nibbling on present thoughts. I'm curious about the
contradiction between his (circle one) tenuous/tenacious
leaning way, and his actual choice of words. Our guts are
involved, our customary expressions buffeted by currents. We
navigate potential space, but neither of us can see our event
horizon. Shame is guarded by ___________. He wonders
if he can sustain love, and what he took as evidence of love
from his mother. He knows, in a formless way, why his father
___________.

He doubts anyone cares about his smaller wounds. He wants
to rest by a fallen tree near a quiet creek. I sense a surge of his
enigmatic ___________. It hits me as a glaring theme in my
own life. We feel an uneasy recognition, but I must remem-
ber; his path is not mine. I'm careful not to comment when
he needs to freely roam. Gender follows us from past genera-
tions. We fight the categories. He's been looking intently at
the ___________, tucked away in my bookshelf. By now, it's
acquired a private meaning.

I'm looking for a missing chapter. He reports an urgent need
to see ___________. He's reluctant to tell me, says he's much
better anyway. A squall is on the horizon. I try to protect the
space we've worked to create. He speaks of ___________for
the first time. We're deep in this mysterious business. We'll
meet again on Thursday night, but if the moon is full and
orange, we'll speak of little else.

Under the Great Gray Sky

A couple walks down their driveway holding two sides of a
box they're throwing out, too heavy for either to lift alone.
It's filled with the woman's collection of pottery. Every
piece has been methodically broken and she won't say why.
Yesterday, she lined them up in in her backyard, named them,
and crushed them with rocks she brought from the riverbed.
She loves the rocks, the layers and patterns, the millions of
years in her mind. She loves the smooth surfaces, the clarity
of freezing water in winter, witnessed by the great gray sky.
When they're wet, she sees their complexity, their beautiful
striations. That's when she chooses them – not when they're
dry and pale in the blistering heat of summer. In summer, she
loves them differently, at midnight, when they're warm but no
longer hot. She places one against her cheek, closes her eyes,
and thinks of their endurance.

Miguel

At most the boy was five
tagging behind his mother
on a crowed dusty sidewalk

with poverty all around.
His sister climbed from her
stroller, taking a terrible fall.

I saw his tattered clothes, shoes
with holes, as he ran to lift
her up. Her tears became

a river, her cry would soon
unfold. He knew just how
to hold her, in strokes and a

little song, until her suffering
was none. I took tender notice,
praising him with my eyes.

His mother was a fountain
flowing to him in Spanish
with kisses for his crown;

Some of us heard her song.
Miguel, Miguel, mi hijo,
Miguelito, my son.

Mowing the Lawn with Dad

I didn't like the chore. Every Saturday since I was twelve,
it was my job to run the power mower and edger.
My father looked forward to it, would sing or whistle
an Irish tune, free from his week of covering the news,
putting away the sorrows of our small city: the fire where
a family died, the courts, city hall, the gang fights.

We mowed the lawn together. When we were done,
I swept the remaining dirt and grass into a pile.
Pebbles were in there too, thrown up by the edger; the
vicious blade carved a fresh groove in the dirt every time.
Sometimes the rocks would hit my legs and I'd bleed
a little, which he noticed privately. I'd make adjustments
to the metal guard so the rocks would miss me and sail
into the street. He saw me doing that, without instruction,
and kept on whistling or singing, loving the time together.

It's true, I wanted to be playing ball with friends. I stopped
complaining when he told me about the so-called Doctrine
of the Four Winds, where, in the end, after all the work,
we faced the pile of debris together. I thought he'd make me
get the dustbin out, and put every last blade of grass
in the trash. That's what his father made him do. Instead,
he said to sweep a little bit of the pile in each of the four
directions, until all of it was gone. That was his favorite
ending to the day's work. He said the earth absorbs
our imperfections. I did it my own way, as a person must,
but I remember his style of sweeping, with a little anger
in the final thrust of the broom. My way was to pause
after I made the four ritual strokes, leaning on the broom,
smiling at nothing in particular. He never said I should
do it his way. All he said was to give the winds their due.

Path of the Favored Leaf

When children play in leaves
I'm drawn to the reticent ones
living in uninvited dreams
inventing chants and prayers
but even these can't free the boy
from the thick tangles of this world.

His thin hands reach to touch
the thing held sacred in his pocket.
It's captured him; you can't know it
by name; it's the thing that makes
you cry, full of burden and hope.

The girl nearby knows all this,
has named it his obsession.
She knows he fears the leaves
and watches from a distance.
Besides, he has to guard the thing
he dare not speak about, and she
can't help but love him. His weight
must rest on one leg, protecting
the world from monsters.

She leans against the cottonwood,
never telling of her wish for dawn.
She draws the soul of morning
in her notebook, page after page
in variations, having no better love.

Instead, she combs her dusty hair
like the waves she saw at the ocean;
her one visit to the ocean. Her socks
were wet from tumbling waves
chasing the edge of the world.

It was a sapphire moment and nobody
was watching. Her footprints were
swept to sea, and it made her mad
so she came at the ebb to make them
appear again, in a stand with eternity.

Now she sees her beloved waves
migrating in the night, carried by
sandhill cranes. She's haunted by
their calls and craves an upward fall.

Every white moving thing opens
this path to her. She'll be the most
observant woman you'll know,
curious about death, buoyant
in clouds, frowning in midday.

You know another nearby soul,
the one with a grin and a nod,
pretending to be the earth itself,
full of rise and fall, sifting her days
through an endless maze of fables.

Some of us reach for single leaf,
holding the part where the stem
severed from the tree – its path
made fresh by resolute eyes. Hold it
against the sky; the branch is now
your arm, elders have always known,
the leaf is the gift of self.

A door opens and everyone comes
inside. There's soup and bread
and warmth from a comforting fire.
Open the stained page of the book
where you hid your favored leaf.

It falls and you start to catch it,
but it longs for the open air. What
shall we make of this shuddering?

Women on a Bench

You know by furtive glances
they're new and tentative,
relishing some manner of risk,

not knowing where the train
is headed. Sparrows find them
doubting. There's such an art

to this, a hundred variations:
soft focus, greyscale, the turn
of a key, the exquisite decision.

The sun is fast declining.
The sycamores demure.
San Francisco fog arrives,

making them silhouettes.
It's Sunday on the concourse
after a concert in the park.

They rise and start to walk.
A kiss is almost given.
The tall one starts to laugh.

Wish of the Baker's Wife

Release me to the wolves
So I might run among them
Heavy in our winter coats
When breath is hot

And the hunt is on.
Release me from a body
That withers, unable to run.
I have no more words

For what I've become
And would chase a chance
To leave this form, chase it
Through a sharp tangle

Of blackberries, past the lake
And beyond. I hear a call
So clear and pure I'll find
the trail in soft white snow.

For Alison Balsom and the Scottish Ensemble

Violas held the moonrise back
While cellos took the stairs
Grace notes from the violins
Were Anna's hummingbirds.

Handel hid in a cello bow
And made the world allegro.
Taste this beauty, now we know
The earth shall pause for *C.*

A gentle christened breath arose
From the trumpeter dressed in red –
In an octave for a better world
She filled our souls, and yet –

Unraveled were the bass notes
Undressed was harmony
Undone was our composure
In the key of heavenly.

Moonrise

Moonrise
startled me;
orange globe
over a neighbor's
roof. It took me
from my chores,
asked nothing,
gave perspective,
as if distance
is merely
a riddle.

It rose above
the oaks, changed
from orange to
wedding white
and was slightly
on the wane.

It's not that
closer things
were calling.
The clouds last
month were
dense and gray
and I wasn't
expecting you
this way.

I remember
summer, when
you were new
with crescent,
wrapped around
my shadows
in a kiss that
owned the night.

Bring your bright
persuasion. Show
me once again,
the passing ways
of seasons, the
constancy of stars.

Butt-Call on Speakerphone at Starbucks

Cindy, is that you? It's been a while.
Don't tell me this is a pocket call.

Go ahead, say it; I'm a butt-call to you,
nothing else (giggles).

No, seriously. These things are driven
by the unconscious.

Whatever! Since you're here, Trish
dumped Joe for her Yoga teacher.
I wasn't sure if you knew.

I'm not surprised. She's impulsive,
and the teacher is a well-known player.
He's married and Trish didn't know.
Can you believe it? I heard it lasted
two weeks, then Trish confronted him
in front of his students. It's on Utube.
I can't believe you haven't seen it.

Best justice ever. I heard that Trish
tried to get back with Joe. He called her
a slut, said he'd rather masturbate
than ever touch her again. Just think,
he was going to propose to her!

They could use our friendship more
than ever. Don't you see the suffering?

I thought you couldn't stand Joe
after his snarky tweets, and Trish
is about as deep as a rain puddle.

I wonder what you say about me
when you butt-call someone else?

I'm sorry, but I'm not sure why.

I've gained thirty pounds?

I don't trust anyone anymore.

Yeah, it happens. I've become
bitter and sarcastic. The truth is,
I hate my body too.

*Well, it must be catching. I've been
crying for no reason. Look at us,
criticizing one minute, apologizing
the next.*

Listen, I'm going to a new vodka bar
after work. Would you like to come?
My cell is dying. Yes or no, quick!

I don't think I have anything to say.

Of course you do. Please, join me.
I miss the me in you.

(phone goes dead, battery is depleted)

This Rush of Quail

Now this rush of quails
in a waterfall from trees
searches for scattered seeds
as if a gossamer veil
descended; they swiftly sail
while I, unseen, would free
myself from fourteen keys
tossed on a pile of mail.

Deep in my lair, a spinning chair;
I'm lost in there and need to find
the carefree ways they take to air
and leave my little yard behind;
quick and skittish, without a care
I'll follow them in my mind.

Eulogy with Paper Lamps

There's a place between lovers
where words refuse all meaning.

We've tried bringing water,
clarification, patience, amnesty,

and the honesty we owe. I propose
a vigil, at night at river's edge,

a eulogy for the unsaid,
sending candles downstream

in separate paper lamps. The eddies
can have them; carnival lights

rounding the island tip, not a race
to the sea, no favoring prophesy,

only the best we can do tonight:
kind, raw, necessary. We'll take

different paths home, hands stuffed
in winter coats, our breath in January

vanishing in tiny clouds. I'll see you
in the morning. I'll split the firewood

then. We're lovers through a window.
You, with your crochet hooks, mending.

An Excellent End of Everything

When everything here is done
a childhood friend comes waltzing
through the almond orchard, swinging
an empty pail. How can it be? You're
eighty-three in a nursing home,
sipping oxygen down a sterile hall.

You saw her last when you were ten.
She whispered your willing eyes to sleep
and laid with you in summer grass
until a whimsy breeze made her touch
your perfect cheek with a pale
fallen leaf, just to see you wake.

The ocean was in her eyes, plum soft hands.
It was then you told her, and no one else,
where you hid your treasures. Drift if you
must - but mirrored on the polished floor
a child dares the wind. She's come
again to race you to the lone blue oak

in the middle of the orchard. Of course
she remembers all you ever told her.
She's come to fill her pail with your life
collection of smooth round rocks, stones
for skipping, a piece of petrified wood,
and other boyhood treasures.

The Final Wish of Elizabeth Mars

From the short story by J.L. Cooper, "A Final Case for Elizabeth Mars"

Release me to the wolves
So I might run among them
Heavy in our winter coats
When breath is hot

And the hunt is on.
Release me from a body
That withers, unable to run.
I have no more words

For what I've become
And would chase a chance
To leave this form, chase it
Through a sharp tangle

Of blackberries, past the lake
And beyond. I hear a call
So clear and pure I'll find
the trail in soft white snow.

About the Author

J.L. COOPER was an author and psychologist in Sacramento, California. His writing highlights the lyricism in everyday life, relational mysteries, and the elevation of subjective experience. He has received five literary awards in fiction, nonfiction, poetry, and essay, including the *Tupelo Quarterly Prose Open Prize*, TQ9, judged by Pulitzer winner Adam Johnson, and the Grand Prize in Poetry, *Crosswinds Poetry Journal*, 2018, judged by Pulitzer winner in criticism Lloyd Schwartz. His full-length book of poetry, *An Ocean Large Enough* (David Robert Books) is available on Amazon Books, as are his two books of short stories, *The Sages of 47th Street* and *A Perfect Stillness*, and a novella, *Spell of the Pelicans*. His short stories, poetry and a craft piece have appeared or are forthcoming in numerous journals including *The Manhattan Review, The Comstock Review, New Millennium Writings, Oberon Poetry Magazine, Story Quarterly, Cutthroat, Hippocampus, Leveler, The Tishman Review, 3Elements Review, Structo,* and several other journals and anthologies. His website is: jlcooper.net.

James passed away at home with his family in October, 2018 after a 5-year battle with cancer. This is his final book.

Also by J.L. Cooper

Available through Amazon, Barnes & Noble,
Book Depository, and most online book retailers.

PO Box #3092
Citrus Heights, CA 95611-3092
fivewarblers.wordpress.com

www.ingramcontent.com/pod-product-compliance
Lightning Source LLC
Chambersburg PA
CBHW032132050726
47590CB00008B/3051